FOSS Science Stories

Measurement

Developed at
Lawrence Hall of Science
University of California at Berkeley

Published and Distributed by **Delta Education**

ISBN-10: 1-58356-837-9
ISBN-13: 978-1-58356-837-8
542-2004

7 8 9 10 11 12 QUE 13 12 11 10 09 08

TABLE OF CONTENTS

A ROYAL MEASUREMENT MESS

Many years ago, in a place far away, lived a boy named Rakim. Rakim lived with his family in a cottage on the edge of a pasture. Each morning, Rakim and his father left the cottage to tend the sheep in the pasture. Rakim's brother was a furniture maker. He made wood into beautiful chairs and tables. Rakim's sister delivered the villagers' milk. Each day, she milked and tended the family cows.

One afternoon, Rakim's sister returned from the village. She held up a piece of paper for the entire family to see.

"Agbar, our new king, demands that every family give gifts to him," she said. "Our family must give one stone's worth of wool, two pitchers of milk, and a chair that is six hands high. We have only a week to prepare these gifts."

Over the next few days, Rakim's family prepared their gifts. Rakim and his father sheared the sheep each morning and packed the wool into two big bags each evening.

"Father, how will we know when we have enough wool?" Rakim asked.

"I use the stone sitting in Mother's garden to estimate how much to give," his father replied. "That stone is about the same size as the king's royal measurement stone. I lift up the stone, then I lift the two bags. When they feel about the same heaviness, I know we have enough wool."

After the wool was ready, Rakim helped his brother measure the chair using a stick. "This stick is equal to the king's royal hand," Rakim's brother told him. Rakim held the stick against the chair. "It's just six hands!" his brother exclaimed.

The next day, Rakim and his family were to appear before the new king. Rakim's sister arose extra early to milk her cows. She came from the barn carrying two pitchers. They were equal to the royal pitchers the king had always used.

"Those should please the king well," Rakim's mother told her. "Now let's be off."

Soon they arrived at the palace. They were led to a large room where the young king sat accepting his gifts.

Rakim's father did not look happy. He was looking at the king's sour-faced gift collector. The gift collector was known as a dishonest fellow. However, the old king had made sure the gift collector had treated the people fairly.

Rakim's brother and sister placed their gifts in front of the king. Finally Rakim's father set down the bags of wool.

The king looked at the gifts. "These gifts are—" he began.

"Small, indeed!" cut in the gift collector. "Are you trying to cheat your new king?" He turned to a nearby soldier. "Bring out the king's measures!" he demanded.

Shortly two soldiers staggered in carrying a large boulder between them. Another followed with a stick. One more man came in holding a colossal container.

"Here is the measure for the new king's hand," the gift collector barked, pointing at the stick. "And here are his stone and his pitcher." He pointed at the huge rock and the enormous jug. "Take the head of this family to the dungeon," he ordered.

Rakim became very angry. "Wait! This is *not fair!*" he shouted.

"Your gifts are too small!" said the gift collector. "The new king uses new measurements."

"These new measurements are much bigger than the last king's!" Rakim said. "None of the people in the village will be able to give the king his gifts using these measurements!"

"Enough!" shouted Agbar. He turned to Rakim and stared at him. Finally he spoke.

"Rakim is right. These measurements are unfair." The gift collector's jaw dropped. "From now on, Rakim will be my new gift collector." He looked at the amazed boy. "You will create standard measures that will be used in this kingdom for all time. We will need a standard stone for weighing, a standard hand for measuring length, and a standard pitcher for measuring volume. Place copies of these measurements in the center of the village for all people to use. From now on, all measurements will be fair and unchanging."

So Rakim, the new Royal Gift Collector, found a stone that was heavy, yet not too heavy for one man to lift alone. Next he cut a stick that was exactly the length of Agbar's hand. Then Rakim used his sister's largest pitcher to measure liquids.

And that is how many years ago, in a place far away, standard measurements came to be created.

THE METRIC SYSTEM

The metric system is a very easy system of measurement to use. Can you multiply and divide by tens? Then you can use the metric system!

Measurement systems based on multiples of ten were proposed many times in history. In 1793, people in France created the metric system. The French based this system of measurement on a unit they called the *meter.* Meter comes from the Greek word *metron,* which means "measure."

North Pole
10,000,000 meters
Equator

How did the French set the size of a meter? They made the meter one ten-millionth of the distance from the North Pole to the equator. They wanted the meter to be based on a unit that would never change. The meter was then used to create other metric units. These units of mass and volume are the *gram* and the *liter.* Over time, the meter has been reset to be more accurate. It was reset most recently in 1983. Now the meter is based on how far light travels in a vacuum in a tiny fraction of a second.

Metric Prefixes

All metric units are based on the meter.
The *prefix,* or the part of the word that comes first, can help you tell how big a metric unit is.

micrometer	=	0.000001 (one-millionth) of a meter
millimeter	=	0.001 (one-thousandth) of a meter
centimeter	=	0.01 (one-hundredth) of a meter
decimeter	=	0.1 (one-tenth) of a meter
meter	=	1.0 meter
dekameter	=	10.0 meters
hectometer	=	100.0 meters
kilometer	=	1,000.0 meters
megameter	=	1,000,000.0 meters

Metric Measures

The *meter* is the basic unit of length in the metric system. The *gram* is the basic unit of mass. The *liter* is the basic unit of volume.

Meter A meter is approximately the distance from a doorknob to the floor.

millimeter = one-thousandth of a meter
centimeter = one-hundredth of a meter
kilometer = 1,000 meters

Gram A nickel weighs about 5 grams.

milligram = one-thousandth of a gram
kilogram = 1,000 grams

Liter A liter is the amount of liquid in a 1-liter soda bottle.

milliliter = one-thousandth of a liter

An elevation sign, in both meters and feet

The metric system slowly caught on around the world. Seventeen countries signed the Treaty of the Meter in 1875. This treaty created the International Bureau of Weights and Measures. The bureau adopted the metric system as the worldwide standard of measurement. Today the metric system is the standard everywhere in the world.

Everywhere, that is, except the United States. The U.S. does not use the metric system. It is the only major country in the world that does not use the metric system as its official measuring system. But even in the United States, the metric system is used in many areas. It is used in scientific fields and in the marketplace. It is used in many sports and recreational activities. One day, metrics might be used for every measurement in your home!

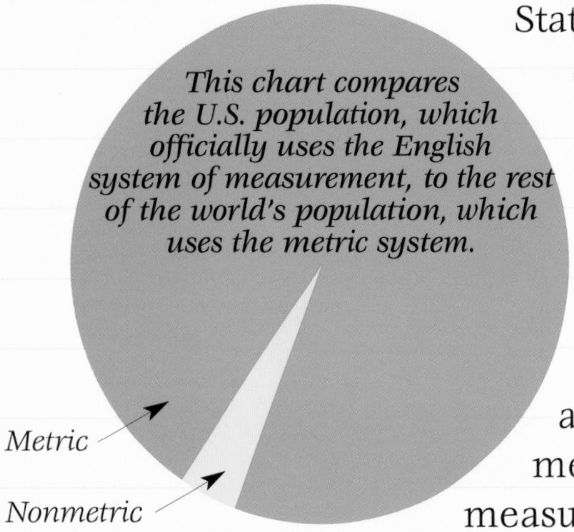

This chart compares the U.S. population, which officially uses the English system of measurement, to the rest of the world's population, which uses the metric system.

Metric

Nonmetric

MEASURE THIS!

Some things are difficult to estimate because they fool your eyes. Things that fool your eyes are called *optical illusions*. Look at each of the optical illusions below. First guess the answer to each question just by looking at the pictures. Then, using a ruler, measure each optical illusion to check your answers.

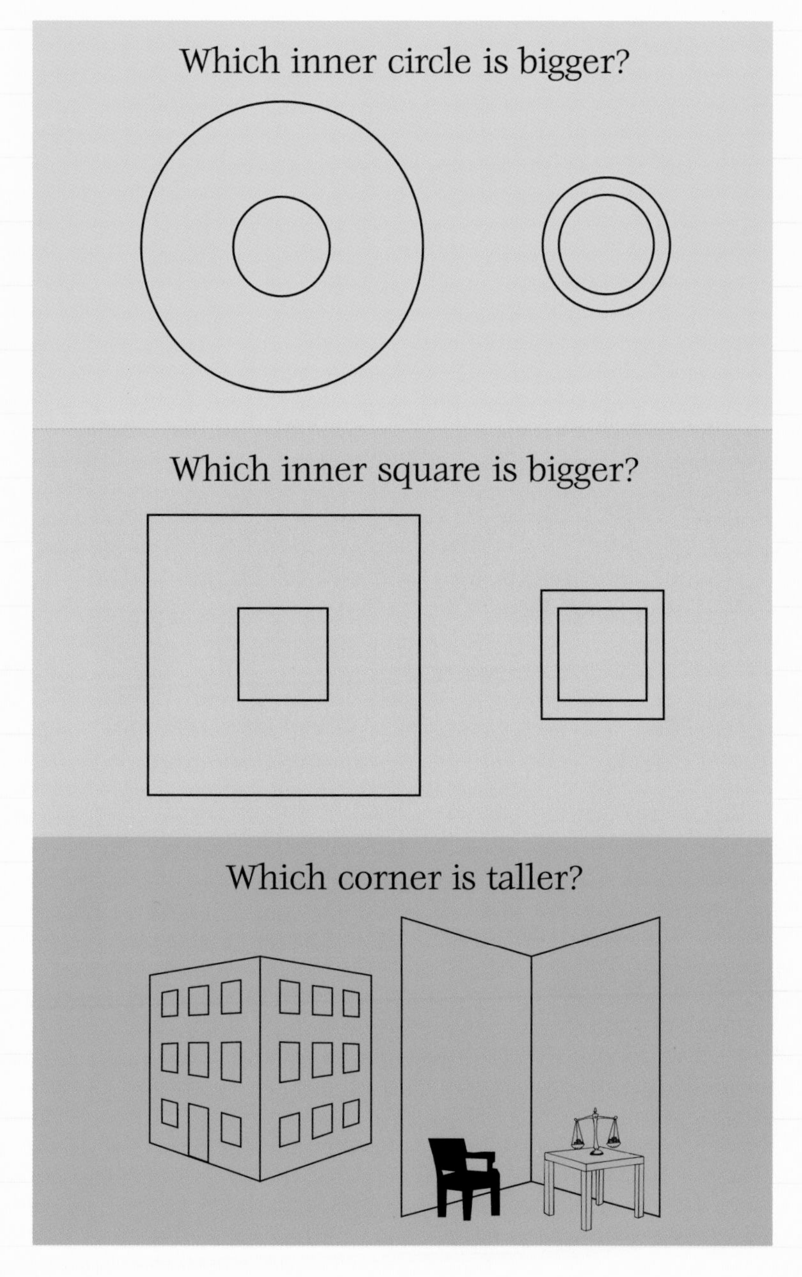

THE METRIC SYSTEM IN THE UNITED STATES

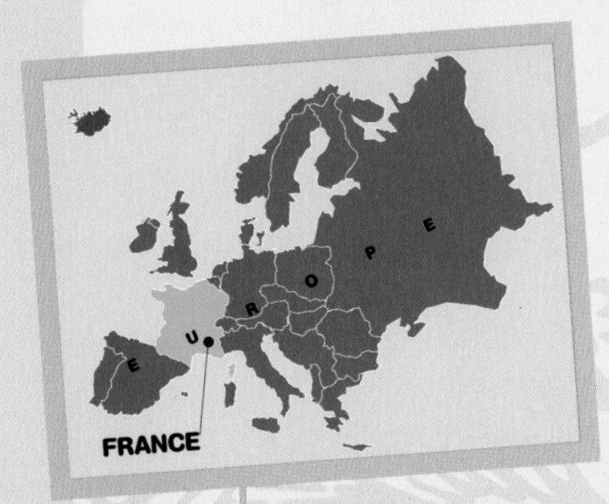

1607

Jamestown in Virginia is settled by colonists from England. The colonists bring the English system of measurement to America.

1793

The metric system is created in France.

1821

John Quincy Adams writes a report praising the metric system. In the report, Adams says that the metric system is nearly perfect. Adams would later become our country's sixth president.

1866

The U.S. Congress passes a bill legalizing the use of the metric system in America. The new bill makes it illegal to refuse to deal in metric units. Some areas of science and industry begin using the metric system.

1873

The U.S. Treasury sets the weight of silver coins using the metric system. The half dollar weighs 12.5 grams. The quarter weighs 6.25 grams. The dime weighs 2.5 grams. The nickel weighs 5 grams. These weights remain the same until 1965. At that time, different metals are mixed in with the silver, which changes the weights.

1875

The United States is one of 17 countries to help found the International Bureau of Weights and Measures. The bureau adopts the metric system as the worldwide system of measurement.

1896

A bill sent to Congress recommends the metric system as the standard system of measurement in the United States. However, most Americans are not ready or willing to switch to metrics. The bill fails to pass. A similar bill in 1902 also fails.

If you think the metric system in the United States is a new idea, think again. In the U.S., the metric system has had supporters for more than 150 years. The metric system was first created in France in 1793.

1960 An updated version of the metric system is approved by the International Bureau of Weights and Measures. The length of the meter is reset.

1965 Great Britain adopts the metric system as its standard system of measurement.

1971 A 3-year report to Congress is finished. The report is called "A Metric America–A Decision Whose Time Has Come." It recommends that America go metric within 10 years.

1975 Congress passes the Metric Conversion Act. This act encourages all Americans to adopt the metric system. A year later, the U.S. Metric Board is set up.

1982 The U.S. Metric Board disbands. The U.S. government thinks it will cost too much to change all businesses and manufacturing to metric measures.

1983 The length of the meter is reset once again. Now the size of the meter is based upon how far light travels in a vacuum in a tiny fraction of a second.

1988 Congress passes an act stating that metrics is the preferred system of measurement for all trade and business. It also requires all government agencies to switch to the metric system. Today all major government agencies have created plans and committees to find the best ways to change to metric measures.

QUESTIONS TO EXPLORE

- How many times have people in the U.S. tried and failed to make the change to the metric system?
- Why do you think Americans do not want to change to the metric system?
- If you were elected to Congress, would you try to pass a law that required people to use metrics, or would you want to keep the English system? Why?

MIND-BOGGLING MEASUREMENTS

One Major Munchie: The world's largest burrito was built in 1997 in Mountain View, California. It was 1,090 meters long! That's about the length of seven city blocks! More than 2,000 kilograms of burrito fixings were used to create this mega-munchie. That's about the mass of 60 fourth graders!

A Weighty Subject: At the 1996 Olympics, Russian Andrei Chemerkin broke a world record by lifting 260 kilograms. That was more than twice his own mass! Chemerkin himself weighed 114.7 kilograms at the time.

Andrei Chemerkin

Teeny, Tiny Creatures: The bumblebee bat is the world's tiniest mammal. It grows to be about 2.5 centimeters. That's about the distance from the tip of your thumb to the first knuckle. The bat's wingspan is about 16 centimeters. Its mass is about 2 grams. That's about as much as a few paper clips. Bumblebee bats are found in Thailand.

Big Blue: The blue whale is the largest living animal. These massive creatures can grow to be 30.5 meters long. They can weigh more than 130,000 kilograms. That's more than the mass of eight school buses!

Outstanding Ostriches: The ostrich is the world's largest living bird. These big birds are found in Asia and Africa. They can grow to be 3 meters tall with a mass of more than 150 kilograms.

Tiny Wonders: The bee hummingbird, found in Cuba, is the world's smallest bird. Its mass is less than 2 grams. It measures just 6 centimeters. That's about the size of your little finger!

MEASUREMENTS THROUGH TIME

Throughout history, people have created systems of measures. Systems of measures help people work, trade, and play.

BODY MEASUREMENTS

Many of the earliest measures were based on parts of the human body. The *cubit,* for example, was created by the Egyptians around 3000 B.C.E. One cubit was the distance from the elbow to the tip of the middle finger. The Egyptians also used measures called the *palm* and the *digit.* Can you guess how they were measured?

WHEN IN ROME

The Romans adopted and changed many measurements used by the Greeks, Babylonians, and Phoenicians. One Roman invention was the *milestone.* This large stone was used to mark a Roman mile. A Roman mile was measured by 1,000 double-step paces.

FEET FIRST

Many cultures used the human foot to measure things. The Greeks divided their foot into 16 units. These were called *fingers.* Later the Romans divided the foot into 12 units. Each one was the width of a thumb. They called these units *inches.*

SEEDS AND OTHER STANDARDS

Early societies used seeds and other farming objects as measures. In 1324, for example, King Edward II created his own standard for an inch. His inch equaled three round, dry barleycorns laid end to end.

TWO DIFFERENT STANDARDS

In many ancient kingdoms around the world, two standards of measurement were used. These were the *royal measure* and the *common measure*. The royal measure was larger than the common measure. When the king was paid his taxes, the royal measure was used. When the king had to pay, however, the common measure was used.

Measurements based on body parts and other methods were not very accurate or fair. Measurements often changed from country to country. They even changed from city to city. These different measurements often caused problems. As trade between cities and nations grew, the need for standard measurements became clear.

Ancient Measurements Used Today

Some measurements we use today had their origins many years ago. Here are a few of these measurements.

Hand The hand was roughly equal to the size of an adult palm. Today the hand is 10.2 centimeters. The hand is used to measure horses. Most horses are 14 to 19 hands high.

Furlong The furlong was originally equal to the distance a horse could plow before it needed rest. Today the furlong is equal to 201 meters. It is commonly used to measure horse races.

Fathom The fathom measures ocean depths. Long ago, a fathom was the distance from one hand to another when a man stretched out his arms. Today it is 1.83 meters.

Knot The knot, or nautical mile per hour, measures the speed of ships. Sailors used to measure the speed of a ship by dropping a knotted rope over the ship's side. They counted the number of knots released every 28 seconds. Today the knot is equal to 1.85 kilometers per hour.

Carat The carat was first used by Arabs to weigh precious metals and stones. Each carat was equal to the mass of a small bean called a *karob.* Today the carat is equal to 200 milligrams. Carats are still used to weigh diamonds and other precious stones.

THE METRIC SYSTEM AT WORK

The United States does not officially use the metric system. Yet the metric system is used by many people here. Some of the first people in America to use the metric system were scientists.

Today scientists around the world use the metric system. The metric system is the international system of measurement. U.S. scientists use it for their research, as well. They use the metric system to measure, compare, describe, and analyze information.

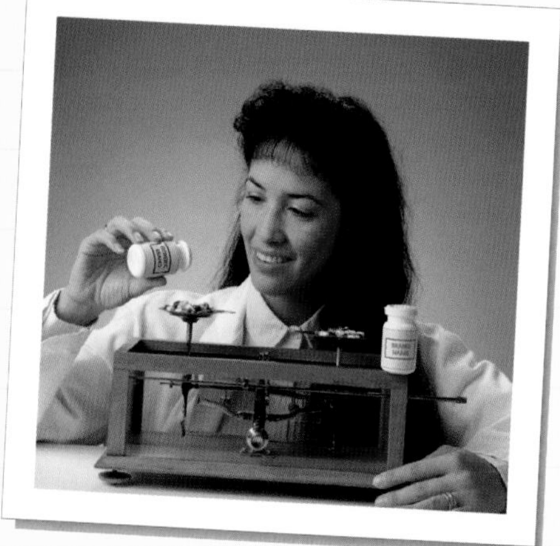

Medicines are carefully weighed by pharmacists to ensure the right dosages.

PHARMACISTS

Today most medicines are measured using the metric system. Pharmacists measure and label all types of medicines using the metric system. On a bottle of aspirin, the dosage is listed in milligrams.

METEOROLOGISTS

Meteorologists study Earth's atmosphere and weather. They use the metric system to measure temperatures and other weather conditions. They also use it to measure the amounts of chemicals in Earth's atmosphere.

Meteorologists use the metric system to gauge and predict weather conditions.

BIOLOGISTS

Biologists study animals and plants. They use the metric system to measure and weigh animals and plants. They also use metrics to map the places plants and animals live. Biologists who work in zoos use metric measures to help them take care of the animals. Like pharmacists, they measure medicines using the metric system.

Astronauts use metric measurements for all their space duties.

ASTRONAUTS

Astronauts are trained to take part in spaceflights. The National Aeronautics and Space Administration (NASA) uses metric weights and measures on all flights.

ECOLOGISTS

Ecologists study the relationships between living things and their environments. They measure how much pollution is being released into Earth's atmosphere and water. They use the metric system for these measurements. Ecologists also use the metric system to measure and map the loss of some environments. This loss is caused by droughts, floods, or other natural disasters.

ARCHAEOLOGISTS

Each new find is carefully measured and recorded by this archaeologist.

Archaeologists study how people lived long ago. They use the metric system when charting and mapping areas they are studying. They also measure and weigh bones and other objects they find using the metric system.

Doses of Medicine

Many years ago, *apothecaries* were people who gave out medicine. They had to use gram masses to help them measure out the exact amounts their customers needed. But a full set of mass pieces was expensive. Apothecaries often found ways to use only a few mass pieces to make many different measurements.

Pretend you have a balance, and use the three gram masses shown below to measure the prescriptions. The prescriptions should weigh from 1 gram all the way up to 13 grams.

WATER EVERYWHERE

It's easy to take water for granted. Water is everywhere. It's the most common substance on our planet. More than 70 percent of our Earth is covered by water. But just a tiny percentage, about one percent, of all Earth's water is fresh water that people can use.

Water is one of our planet's most precious natural resources. All living things need water to survive. In some areas of the world, water is scarce and more valuable than gold. Even in parts of the United States, droughts and water shortages can occur.

How much water do we use?

- Each American uses about 300 to 380 liters of water each day.
- Flushing the toilet uses between 15 and 26 liters each time, depending upon the type of toilet.
- A bath uses about 114 liters.
- A shower uses between 19 and 38 liters per minute.
- Do you leave the water running when you brush your teeth? If so, you use from 3 to 7 liters of water each time.
- A dripping faucet can waste more than 3,800 liters of water each year.

BE A WATER WATCHER

What can you do to conserve water? First pay attention to how much water you use each day. Here are some other tips to help you become a water watcher.

- Keep a pitcher of water in the refrigerator. Then you won't have to run the faucet to get really cold water.
- Try to take short showers instead of baths.
- Use water-saving faucets and shower heads.
- Don't let the water run while you brush your teeth. Also, turn off running water while you soap up your hands.
- Don't throw tissues and other trash into the toilet. Use a trash can instead. This will cut down on the number of times you flush.
- If you have a fish tank, recycle the water by giving it to your plants. The fish-tank water is a good plant fertilizer.

FILL 'ER UP

Get the lowdown on these amazing liquid measurements!

- Elephants need a lot of water. They can drink from 75 to 100 liters each day.
- The average American drinks about 19 liters of orange juice each year. Nine out of every ten Florida oranges are squeezed into juice.
- The average American also eats more than 24 liters of ice cream a year!
- Camels are prized animals in the desert. They can go for long stretches without any water. A camel who has gone without water for a long time can drink 100 liters or more at once.

QUESTIONS TO EXPLORE

- **What things do you do at home to save water?**
- **How could you figure out how much water you would use if you brushed your teeth and left the water running?**
- **About how much water do you drink at one time? In one day? How does that compare to the camel?**

MEASUREMENTS IN THE MARKETPLACE

By learning about standard units of measure, you can be a smarter shopper. All packages, bottles, bags, and cans in a store have important information on their labels. The labels tell exactly how much is inside a package.

Nutrition Facts

Serving Size 2/3 cup (55g)
Servings Per Container 12

Amount Per Serving	
Calories 210	
Calories from Fat 25	
	% Daily Value*
Total Fat 3g	**5%**
Saturated Fat 1g	**4%**
Polyunsaturated Fat 0.5g	
Monounsaturated Fat 1.5g	
Cholesterol 0mg	**0%**
Sodium 140mg	**6%**
Potassium 190mg	**5%**
Total Carbohydrate 44g	**15%**
Other Carbohydrate 23g	
Dietary Fiber 3g	**13%**
Sugars 18g	
Protein 5g	
Vitamin A	0%
Vitamin C	0%
Calcium	2%
Iron	6%
Thiamin	10%
Phosphorus	10%
Magnesium	10%

* Percent Daily Values are based on a 2000 calorie diet. Your daily values may be higher or lower depending on your calorie needs:

	Calories	2,000	2,500
Total Fat	Less than	65g	80g
Sat Fat	Less than	20g	25g
Cholesterol	Less than	300g	300g
Sodium	Less than	2400mg	2400mg
Potassium		3500mg	3500mg
Total Carbo		300g	300g
Dietary Fiber		25g	30g

Calories per gram:
Fat 9 • Carbohydrate 4 • Protein 4

FOOD LABELS

Food labels tell you how many calories, vitamins, grams of fat, and other things are in a food product. A food label contains both English and metric measurements. Where can you find measurements on the food label?

On the food label, "Serving Size" tells how much the average person eats at one sitting. There are two serving sizes on a label. One is a common household measurement such as cups, slices, or pieces. The other is a metric measurement such as grams or milliliters. The rest of the label tells how many grams or milligrams of fat, cholesterol, sugar, and other nutrients are in a food.

GETTING THE MOST FOR YOUR MONEY

Another important shopping tool to use in grocery stores is the *price per unit label.* This label appears on the shelf below each item. The price per unit label tells you how much an item costs. It also tells how much an item costs compared to other items. For example, look at two different-sized containers of the same soda. You can tell which one costs more per milliliter by comparing the price per unit.

Stonegate Elementary News

Paula Brown
Principal

Issue 3
Volume 20

INSIDE THIS ISSUE:

ANGELA AMATO, SCHOOL REPORTER

Hello, Stonegate students! It's me, Angela, your fearless, fact-finding reporter. Today's article is about shopping. I love talking my dad into buying a chocolate cream pie when we go shopping. It's always the highlight of my trip to the grocery store.

YOGURT

Last week I heard two Stonegate students (who shall remain nameless) arguing over whose yogurt was bigger and better. I stepped in to help.

Both yogurts had cost a dollar. One yogurt container was taller and prettier than the other. But when I looked closely, I could see it was a lot thinner, too. We figured out who had the best buy by looking at how much yogurt was in each container. Sorry, Katie, Tyrone was right. (Whoops!)

After I saved the day in the lunchroom, I decided to take a trip to Bart's Grocery Store. I wanted to try to find more packages that might fool an innocent shopper. I had to pick up some shampoo for my big sister. Here's what I discovered.

turn the page

Stonegate Elementary

ANGELA AMATO CONTINUED

SHAMPOO

In the shampoo aisle, I saw a fancy, colorful bottle. I knew Lia would love it! But then I looked at the price. Whoa! It seemed pretty expensive. I compared it with two nearby bottles of shampoo. Here's what they looked like. Which one do you think is the best buy?

Lovely Locks: $5.99
Price per 500 mL = $7.99

Super Clean: $7.00
Price per 500 mL = $3.50

Super Clean (small): $3.50
Price per 500 mL = $4.00

The best buy is the bottle in the middle. How can you tell? You need to look at the price per unit. You can usually find that on the shelf below the product. The bottle in the middle has the lowest price per unit, even though it has the highest price.

SODA

My next stop was the soda section. Dad has to have his Fizzy Pop! But as you can see from the display, Fizzy Pop comes in many different sizes! Hmmm—which one to buy?

Six-pack: $2.39
Price per 500 mL = $0.56

1-liter bottle: $0.79
Price per 500 mL = $0.40

2-liter bottle: $1.09
Price per 500 mL = $0.27

After looking at the price per unit labels, I decided that the six-pack of cans was out of the question. It cost way too much money!

I decided to buy the biggest bottle of Fizzy Pop, the 2-liter size. Even though the 1-liter bottle costs less, you can see that the 2-liter size is the best bargain by far.

That's all for now! Tune in next week when I'll be investigating something new!

Angela

FAHRENHEIT AND CELSIUS

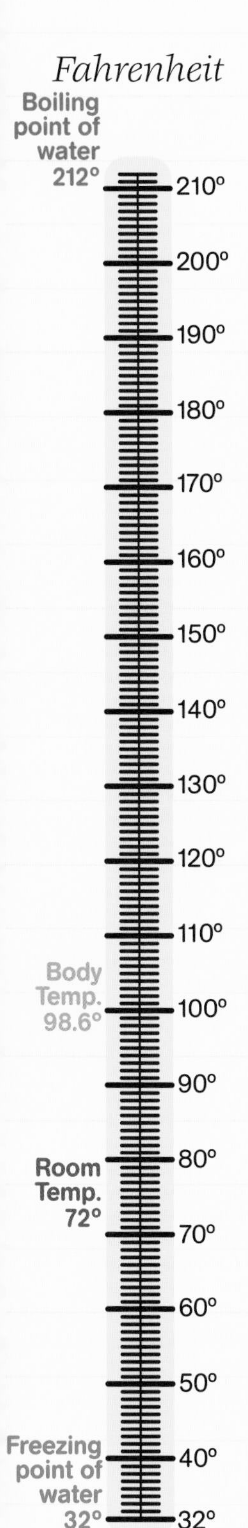

Fahrenheit and Celsius are two scales used to measure temperature. Both scales are based on the freezing and boiling points of pure water at sea level. The Fahrenheit scale has 180° between the freezing and boiling points. The Celsius scale has 100° between the two points.

Today most countries use the Celsius scale to measure temperatures. The United States, however, still uses the Fahrenheit scale.

GABRIEL D. FAHRENHEIT

The Fahrenheit scale is named for German scientist Gabriel D. Fahrenheit. Fahrenheit lived from 1686 to 1736. In 1714, he invented the first mercury thermometer. He invented a temperature scale to go along with it. Fahrenheit's thermometer marked normal body temperature as 98.6°.

Fahrenheit thought he had found the lowest possible temperature by mixing ice and salt. He set the temperature of this mixture at 0°F. Then he set the freezing point of water at 32°F. He also set the boiling point of water at 212°F.

ANDERS CELSIUS

The Celsius scale is named for Anders Celsius, a Swedish astronomer. Celsius lived from 1701 to 1744. In 1742, he created a temperature scale. This scale used 0° to mark water's boiling point and 100° to mark its freezing point. A few years later, another scientist changed Celsius's scale so that 0° was freezing and 100° was boiling. Celsius's scale was originally called the "centigrade" scale. It was renamed in the 1940s to honor the inventor.

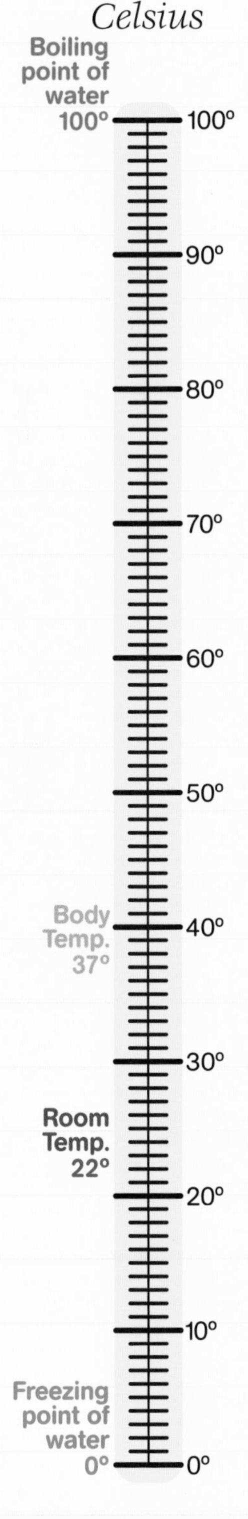

THERMOMETERS

Thermometers are instruments used to measure temperature. There are several different types of thermometers.

CLINICAL THERMOMETER

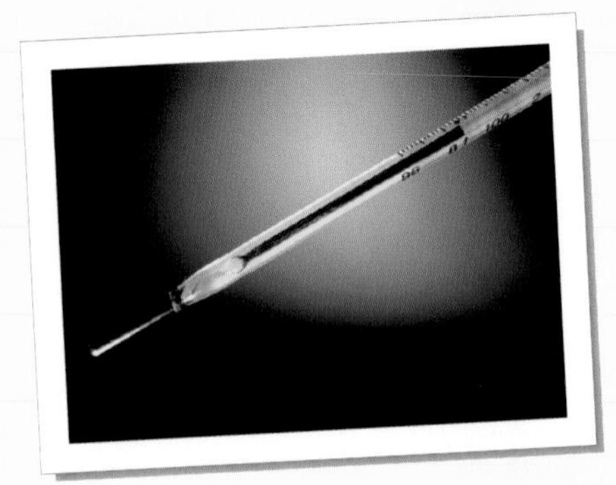

The clinical thermometer is a liquid-in-glass thermometer. A liquid-in-glass thermometer is a glass container filled with liquid. This liquid might be mercury or alcohol. The liquid expands and rises as the thermometer heats up. A clinical thermometer is used to take people's temperatures.

EAR THERMOMETER

Ear thermometers take quick readings of body temperatures when placed in the ear. They measure the heat energy that the ear canal gives off.

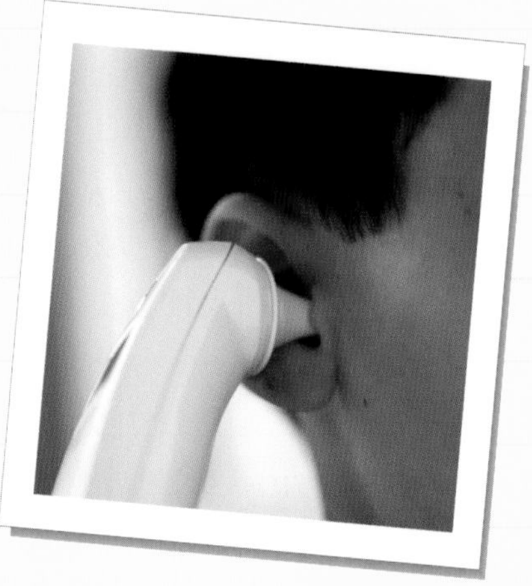

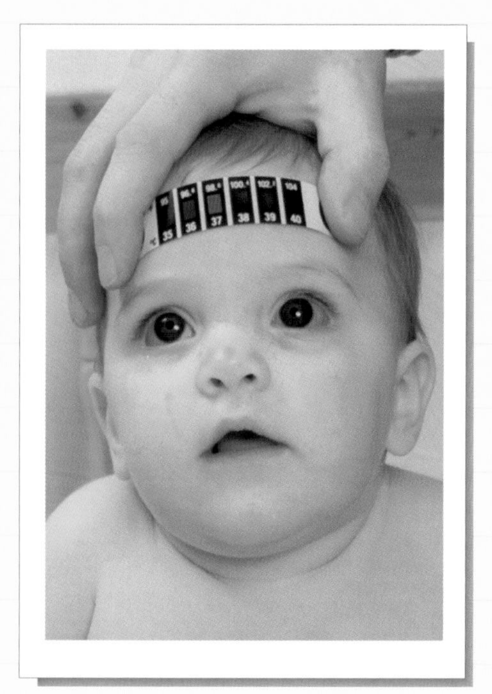

CHEMICAL THERMOMETER

This type of thermometer is a thin plastic strip. It can be placed on a person's forehead to find his or her temperature. These thermometers contain chemicals that melt and change color when heated. They are not the most reliable way to take a person's temperature.

BI-METAL THERMOMETER

A bi-metal thermometer uses two different types of expanding metals to read temperatures. Oven thermometers and refrigerator thermometers are sometimes bi-metal. This type of thermometer is inexpensive. It is not the most accurate thermometer to use.

MAXIMUM-MINIMUM THERMOMETER

A maximum-minimum thermometer is actually two liquid-in-glass thermometers in one. One thermometer contains alcohol. It measures the lowest temperature of the day. The other thermometer contains mercury. It measures the highest temperature of the day.

PYROMETER

A pyrometer measures very hot temperatures, usually over 700°C (almost 1,300°F). Scientists use pyrometers to study the temperatures of lava and other super-hot materials.

RADIOMETER

This thermometer can take temperature readings from far away. A radiometer calculates temperature by measuring the heat energy something is giving off.

Quick Celsius Facts

0°C = Freezing point of pure water (at sea level)
100°C = Boiling point of pure water (at sea level)
22°C = "Room temperature"
37°C = Average body temperature of a human
−26°C = Normal February temperature in Barrow, Alaska
34°C = Normal July temperature in Phoenix, Arizona
16°C = Average global temperature
58°C = Highest recorded global temperature, near Tripoli, Libya, in 1922
−89°C = Lowest recorded global temperature, at Soviet station Vostok in Antarctica in 1983

CAREERS YOU CAN COUNT ON

Every day, people around the world count on accurate measures. They use measurements at home, work, and play. Here are just a few people who use measurements at work.

ATHLETES AND SPORTS OFFICIALS

Many sports use the metric system for measurement. Track and field events, swimming, and skiing are just a few. Runners compete in the 100-, 200-, 400-, and 1,000-meter dashes. Cyclists compete in 10-kilometer races. Divers compete using platforms 10 meters high. That's almost as high as a three-story building!

Athletes often compete against one another in different countries. Because most countries use the metric system, it is used at international sporting events, as well.

Florence Griffith-Joyner finds the right measure for victory.

Amazing Athletic Achievements

These are some world records for international sporting events.

Event	Time/Distance	Record holder	Date
MEN'S TRACK & FIELD			
100-meter dash	9.79 seconds	Maurice Greene, USA	June 16, 1999
200-meter dash	19.32 seconds	Michael Johnson, USA	August 1, 1996
Long jump	8.95 meters	Mike Powell, USA	August 30, 1991
WOMEN'S TRACK & FIELD			
100-meter dash	10.49 seconds	Florence Griffith-Joyner, USA	July 16, 1988
200-meter dash	21.34 seconds	Florence Griffith-Joyner, USA	August 1, 1996
Long jump	7.52 meters	Galina Chistyakova, USSR	June 11, 1988

A skilled chef must measure the right ingredients to prepare a meal.

COOKS

Chefs and bakers use many different types of measurements at work. They need to carefully measure ingredients to use in recipes. Bakers also need to know what temperatures their ovens must be. Then they can cook breads, cakes, and other delicious foods.

CARPENTERS AND ARCHITECTS

Carpenters and architects have to understand many types of metric measurements. They use tape measures, rulers, and other measuring instruments. They also must know how to correctly read *blueprints*. Blueprints are plans that tell exactly what a building will look like.

AUTO MECHANICS

Auto mechanics who work on cars from other countries must know the metric system. Instruction books and packaging materials from other countries may use only metric measurements. This also is true of some parts used to repair foreign cars and trucks.

Mechanics must use metric tools to repair foreign cars.

Veterinarians use the metric system to measure the growth of animals.

VETERINARIANS

Veterinarians use the metric system to measure medicine for animal patients. They also use temperature measurements to see how healthy their patients are.

TEACHERS

Science and math teachers help students learn about the metric system. Nearly all other nations of the world use the metric system. That is why it is important for people in the United States to understand and feel comfortable with the metric system.

You and the Metric System

Would you believe that you use the metric system already? You use it every single day.

- When we talk about electricity, we talk about *watts.* Watts are metric units.
- We buy liters of soda.
- We measure medicine and vitamin dosages in milligrams.
- We use 35-millimeter cameras.

Hunt for Metrics!

Can you find five things around your house that have metric measurements on them? Make a list on a sheet of paper!

VACATION AGGRAVATION

THE AUSTRALIAN ARMS

Here's the opera house in Sydney!

January 3

Dear Grandma,
We just arrived in Sydney, Australia. Wow, did
I get a big surprise. I had read that the January
temperatures in some parts of Australia were usually
around 28°. I packed all my warmest winter clothes
after I read that. When I got off the plane, it was
unbelievably hot! I thought it was some kind of weird
heat wave!
I made a BIG mistake. Temperatures in the
northern part of Australia do average 28° in January.
But that's 28°C! That's about 83°F. It turns out that
because Australia is in the southern half of the world,
their summer is our winter. Mom's still pretty mad.
She had to buy me a bunch of shorts and shirts to
wear. She says that's the last time she'll ever let me
pack my own suitcase!

Love,
Ami

SYDNEY • AUSTRALIA

ZOO NOTES

January 5

Hi Grandma,
Today Mom and I visited the Taronga Zoo in Sydney. I couldn't wait to see the Koalas. I had read they weighed 14 Kilograms. That's about 30 pounds. Did you know that Koalas are endangered? Today many live in zoos.

Love,
Ami

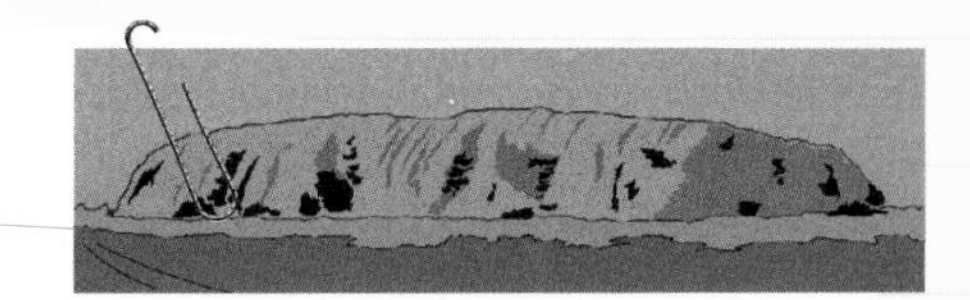

January 8

Hey Grandma,
Today Mom and I visited Ayers Rock. Before I got here, my friend Bill had told me that the rock was 345 feet high. I've climbed that high before, so I was excited to climb Ayers Rock. When we got here, though, Ayers Rock turned out to be 345 meters high! That's over 1,140 feet. We arrived too late in the day to climb to the top, so Mom and I enjoyed the view from the bottom.

Love, Ami

January 10

Hi Grandma,
Today Mom and I took a ride through the Australian countryside. We even saw some Kangaroos. Here's a weird fact. Australians drive on the wrong side of the road. Yup, everyone down under drives on the left. That made me very nervous. When I saw that the speed limit was 100, I got VERY nervous. Then I figured out that 100 Kilometers per hour is only about 62 miles per hour. After that, I could sit back and relax.

Love, Ami

AUSTRALIA

Mrs. Agnes Jones
391 Boston Post Road
Fairfield, CT 06430

Metric to English Conversions

These common conversions might have helped Ami while she was traveling in Australia.

A centimeter is about one-half an inch.
A meter is a little more than 3 feet or 1 yard.
A kilometer is about 0.6 miles.
A kilogram is a little more than 2 pounds.
A liter is about 1 quart.

January 12

G'day, Granny!

Today we checked out one of western Australia's beautiful beaches. It was terrific! And this time, I was prepared. I knew that the water temperature was a warm 20°C (about 68°F). I also knew that the walk to the beach from the hotel was 3 kilometers (1.8 miles). Now that I know that Australia, like most other countries, uses the metric system to measure things, I don't feel so out of place. Mom likes it here, too. In Australia, she only weighs 70 kilograms. (Can you guess how many pounds that is?) See you in a fortnight (that's 2 weeks).

Love,
Ami

QUESTIONS TO EXPLORE

- **If you went to Australia and someone told you it would be 15°C, what clothes would you pack? Why?**
- **If someone told you he or she drank 4 liters of soda with lunch, would you believe him or her? Why?**
- **If you stood on a scale and the number 30 showed on the scale, what unit would you think the scale was measuring?**

EVERYTHING IS MADE OF ATOMS

Two thousand years ago, scholars studied all the materials they could find. They studied solid materials, such as rock, wood, metal, and ice. They studied liquid materials, like water, milk, blood, hot wax, and melted metal. They studied gaslike materials, including air, smoke, steam, and flame. They tried to figure out what each different material was made of.

Scholars thought that all *matter* must be made of only four basic *elements.* They were fire, air, earth, and water. The scholars also thought they could make any kind of material by mixing the right amounts of the four elements.

We now know that fire, air, earth, and water are not the basic elements. Scientists have discovered through experiments that everything on Earth is made out of 92 different elements. Oxygen in the air is one element. The carbon in your pencil is another element. The helium in a party balloon is an element. The *periodic table* shows all the elements in order from the lightest to the heaviest.

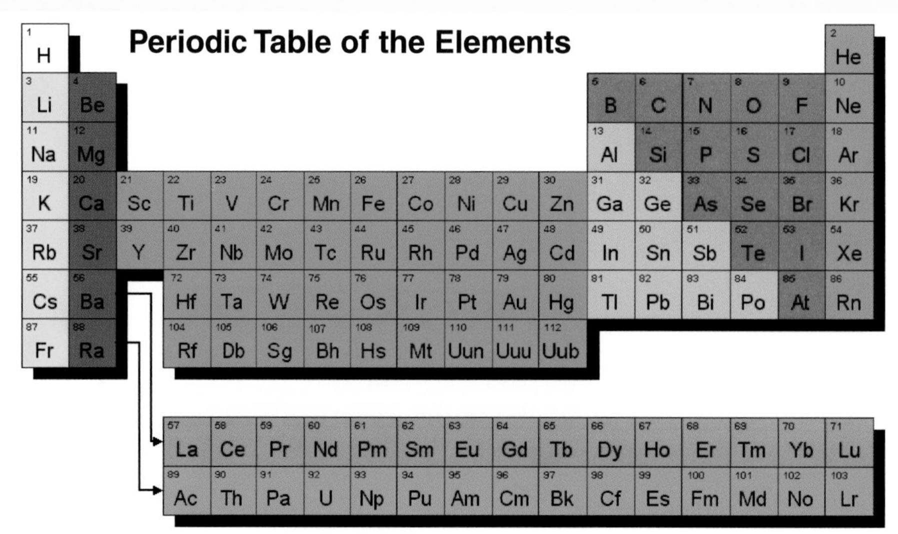

The periodic table shows the 92 naturally occurring elements and the 20 elements created in laboratories by scientists.

Elements are made of tiny particles called *atoms.* An atom is the smallest piece of an element. Each different element is made of its own kind of atom. All matter is made of atoms. But don't bother to look for atoms of oxygen or carbon. Atoms are too tiny to see with your eyes.

MAKING NEW MATERIALS

When atoms of two or more elements combine, they make new materials. The new materials have different properties than the elements from which they are made. Here is an example.

Baking soda and vinegar are two materials made out of elements. A student put solid baking soda in one cup. She put liquid vinegar in another cup.

She put the two cups on one side of a balance, and mass pieces on the other. The system balanced.

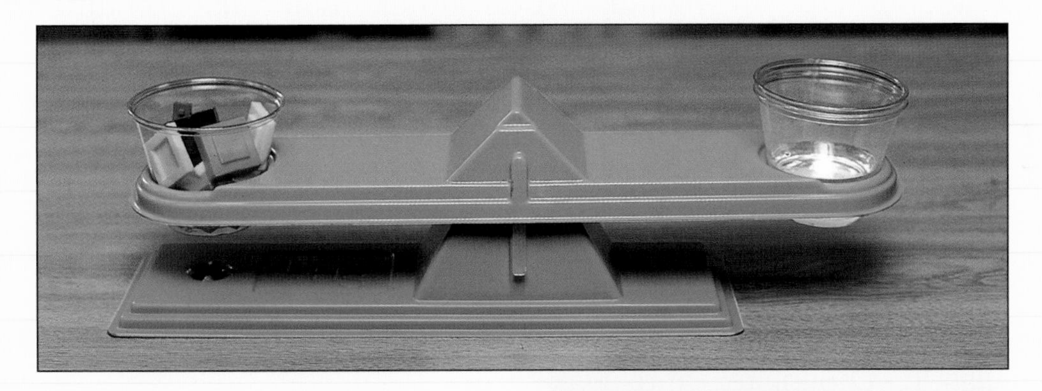

She then poured the vinegar into the cup with baking soda. The vinegar and baking soda fizzed and bubbled.

She put the empty vinegar cup under the bubbling cup. When the fizzing stopped, the system was out of balance. What happened?

The vinegar and baking soda reacted. New materials formed. A gas formed and went into the air. The liquid no longer smelled like vinegar. The white solid material was no longer there.

The gas that formed and went into the air was matter. The gas had mass. When it went into the air, the reaction cup got lighter. When other materials combine, different new materials form. This is how all the materials in the world are made.

CHANGE OF STATE

Matter is found in three forms called *states*. One state is solid. Rock, paper, steel, wood, rubber, plastic, chocolate, and wax are solids. The second state of matter is liquid. Water, oil, milk, gasoline, paint, and dish soap are liquids. The third state of matter is gas. Oxygen, carbon dioxide, helium, and air are gases.

The three states of matter

Some materials change state when they are heated. When materials change from solid to liquid, it is called *melting.* Solid ice changes to liquid water when it melts. Solid butter changes to liquid butter when it melts. Solid metal changes to liquid metal when it melts. What happens when solid candle wax gets hot?

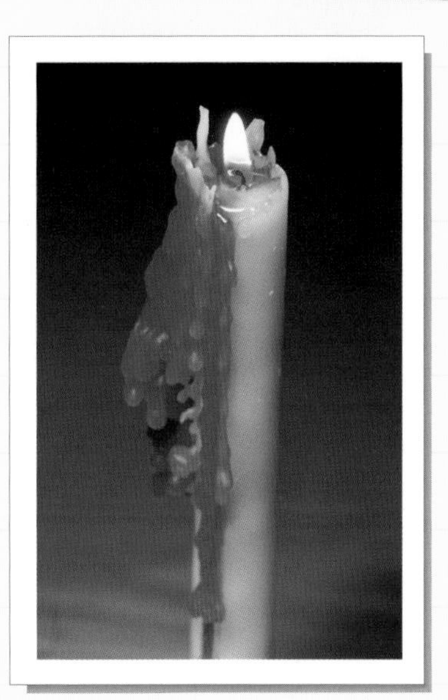

Different materials melt at different temperatures. Ice melts at room temperature. Steel melts in very hot furnaces.

Some materials change into gas when they are heated. When materials change from liquid into gas, it is called *evaporation.* Rainwater evaporates from sidewalks when the Sun comes out. Water evaporates from cooking pots when it boils on the stove. Next time you see a sign that says "Wet Paint," think about what it means. It doesn't mean the paint has water on it. It means the paint is liquid when it is put on the wall. When the liquid evaporates, the solid paint is left behind.

GLOSSARY

Atom The smallest particle of an element. Atoms are the building blocks of matter.

Boiling point The temperature at which water forms vapor.

Degree Celsius (°C) The basic unit of temperature in the metric system. Water freezes at 0 °C and boils at 100 °C.

Element A simple chemical substance that is made of only one type of atom.

Estimate An educated guess about a measurement.

Freezing point The temperature at which water becomes a solid (ice).

Gram (g) The basic unit of mass in the metric system.

Liter (L) The basic unit of fluid volume in the metric system.

Mass A quantity of matter.

Matter The material that everything in the universe is made of. It can be solid, liquid, or gas.

Meter (m) The basic unit of distance or length in the metric system.

Metric system A system of weights and measures based on multiples of ten.

Scale Something divided into regular spaces as a tool for measuring.

Standard measurements Units agreed upon and used by a large number of people.

Temperature A measure of how hot or cold something is.

Thermometer A tool used to measure temperature.

Volume Three-dimensional space.

Weigh To find the mass of. You weigh an object to find its mass.